I0484347

Art Portfolio

Cherie Roe Dirksen

My inspiration...

My art reflects how I interpret the world around me. It is how I see this life ~ a palette of unbelievable colours and a sea of energy. The potential every living thing has and the knowing that everything is a manifestation of divine will, is in itself, pure magic. This is what I want to create - a magical world - for myself and for all those who wish to play in my dream for a while.

I love to travel, especially when I get to visit foreign countries. This gives me the opportunity to soak up different cultures, colours, energy and all the awesome wonders of Gaia.

My native continent, Africa, is my main source of creative expression. Her multiplicity of landscapes, seas, sunsets, forests, deserts, animals and plant species is breathtaking. I am never left for lack of inspiration when I am at home - any artists dream.

I hope you can feel the energy, vibrancy, wonder and beauty I feel when I paint.

~ Cherie Roe Dirksen

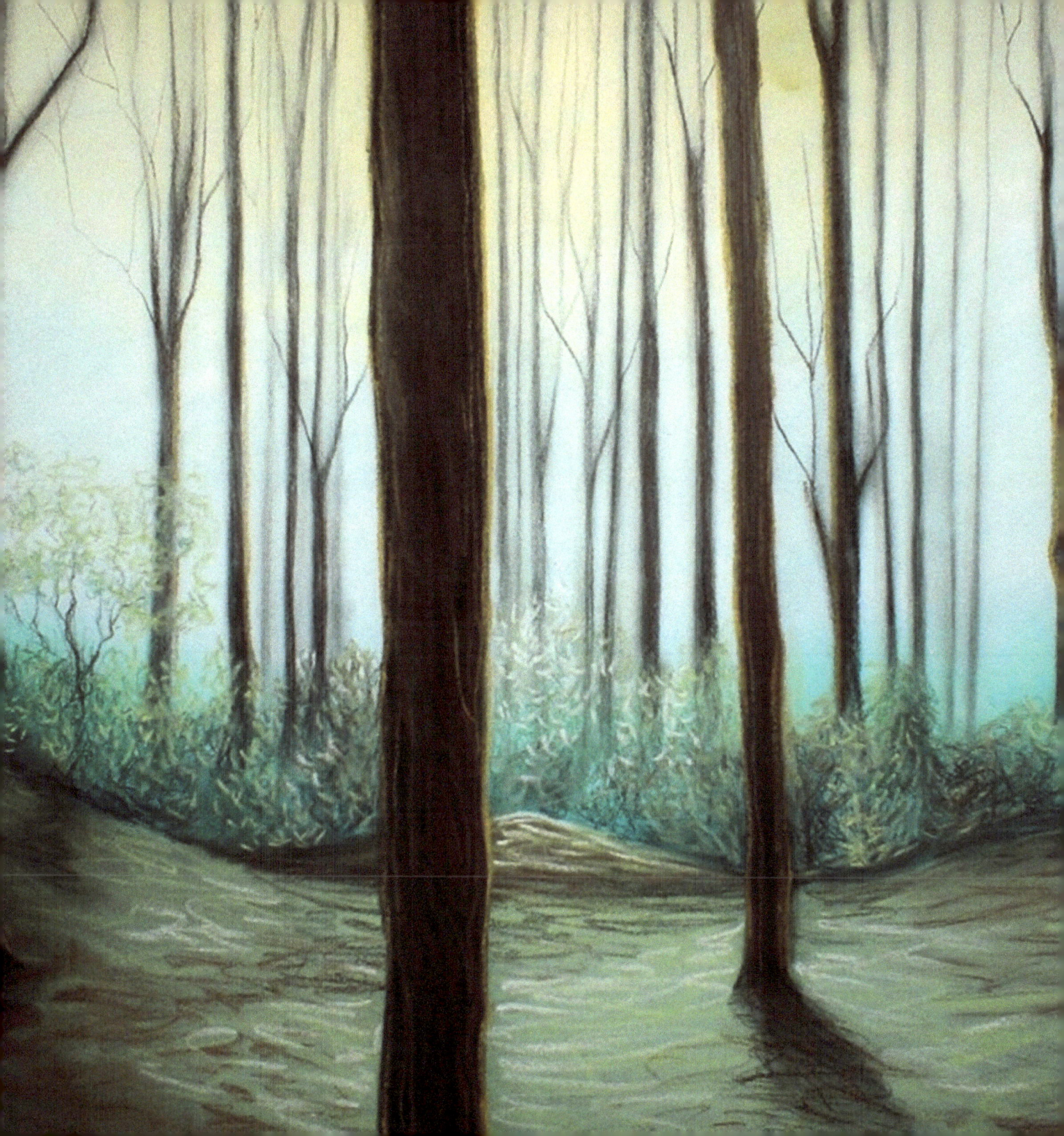

FLOWERS

When I paint a flower I feel an overwhelming bliss - an excitement to capture the beauty and magic of what I see and feel when I am in their glorious presence. I am never happier than when I have a house full of flowers and the scent hangs on the air. Or when I am in my garden just being present with the smell of lavenders on the breeze.

The first category of this portfolio is flowers. They are my main source of inspiration because I still cannot fully fathom their exquisite beauty. Eckhart Tolle put it in a nutshell when he said that we could look upon flowers as the enlightenment of plants. I could look upon flowers all day and stll be mesmerized. They are a true gift to us and to gaze upon their delicate wonder is to look at the unfolding of pure potential.

Delicate bursts of colour, pattern and infinite grace all governed by sacred geometry. Perfectly woven into the fabric of our existence to brighten up our world.

Next time you pass a flower, stop and really look at it. Look deep into it's complex centre. Feel the magnificence of creation and know that there is divine order in everything.

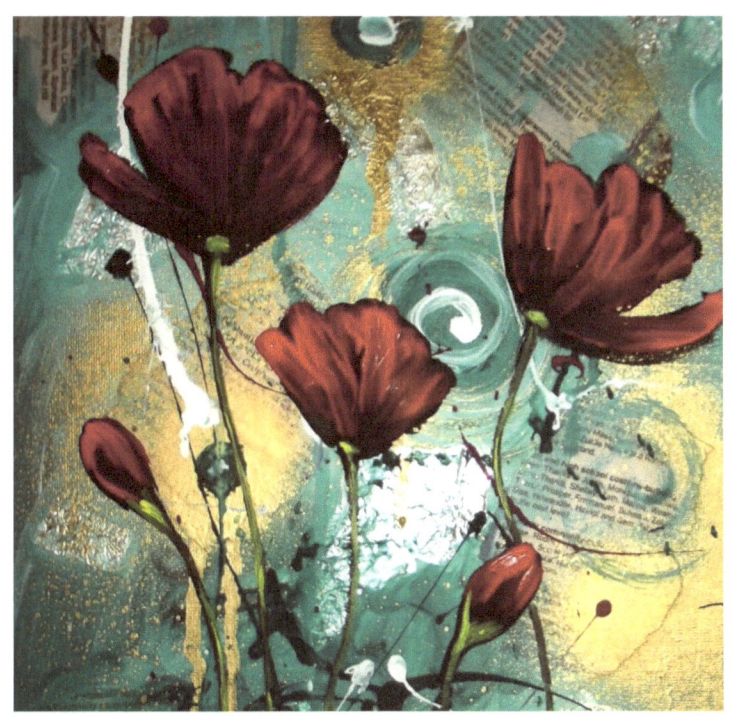
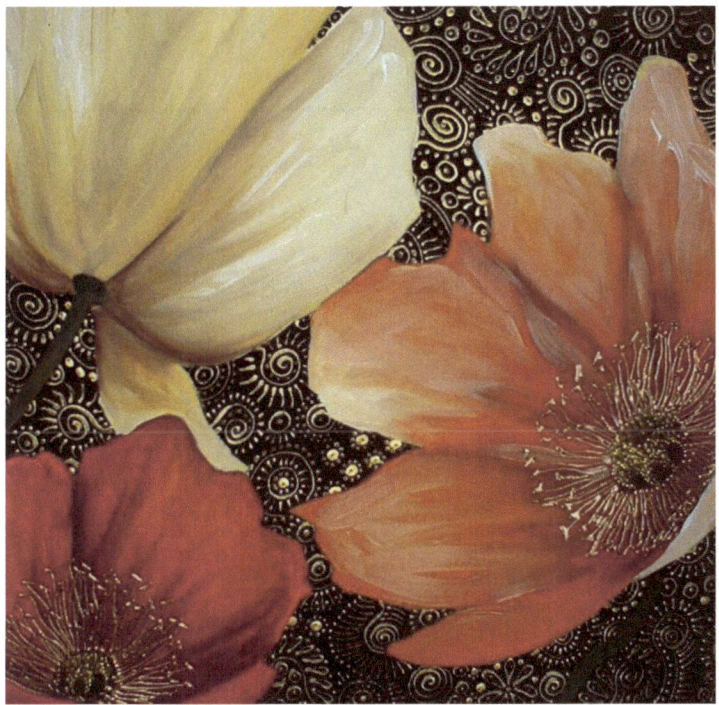

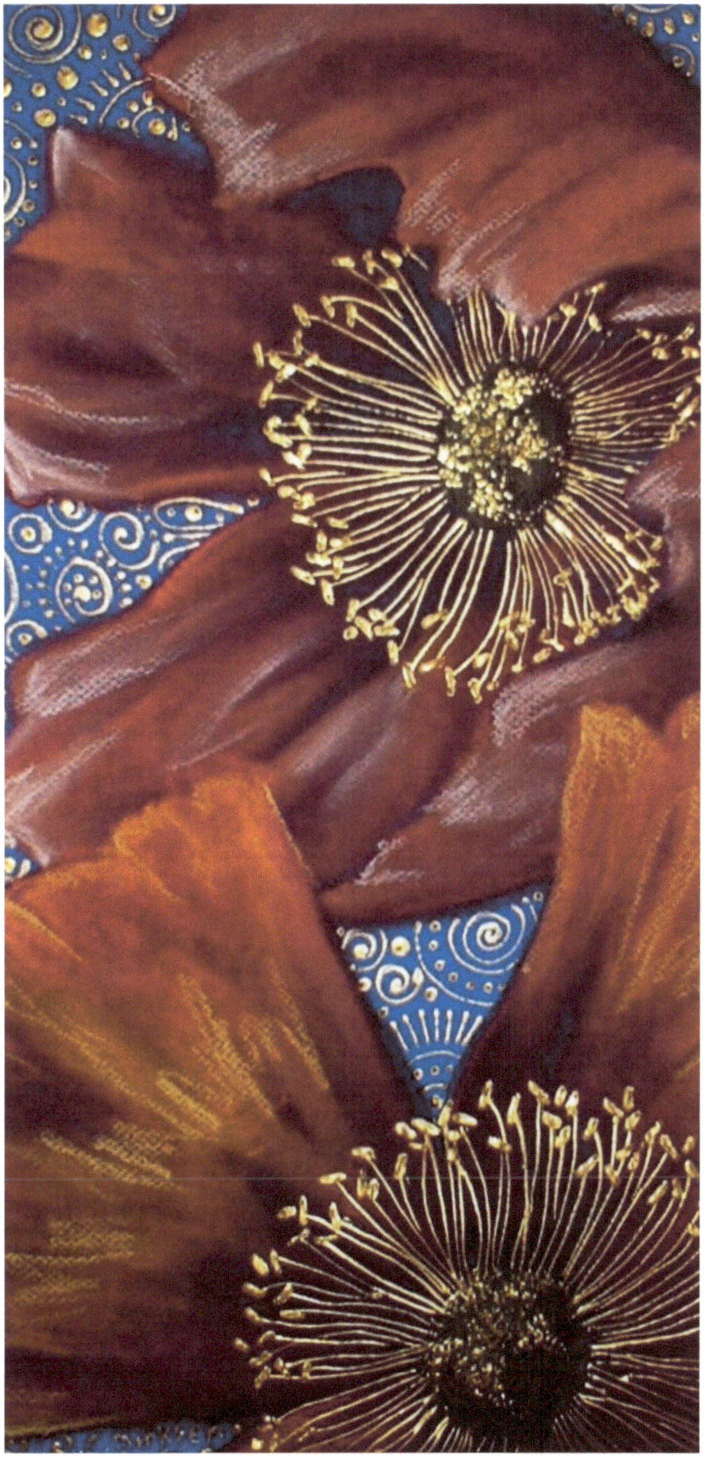

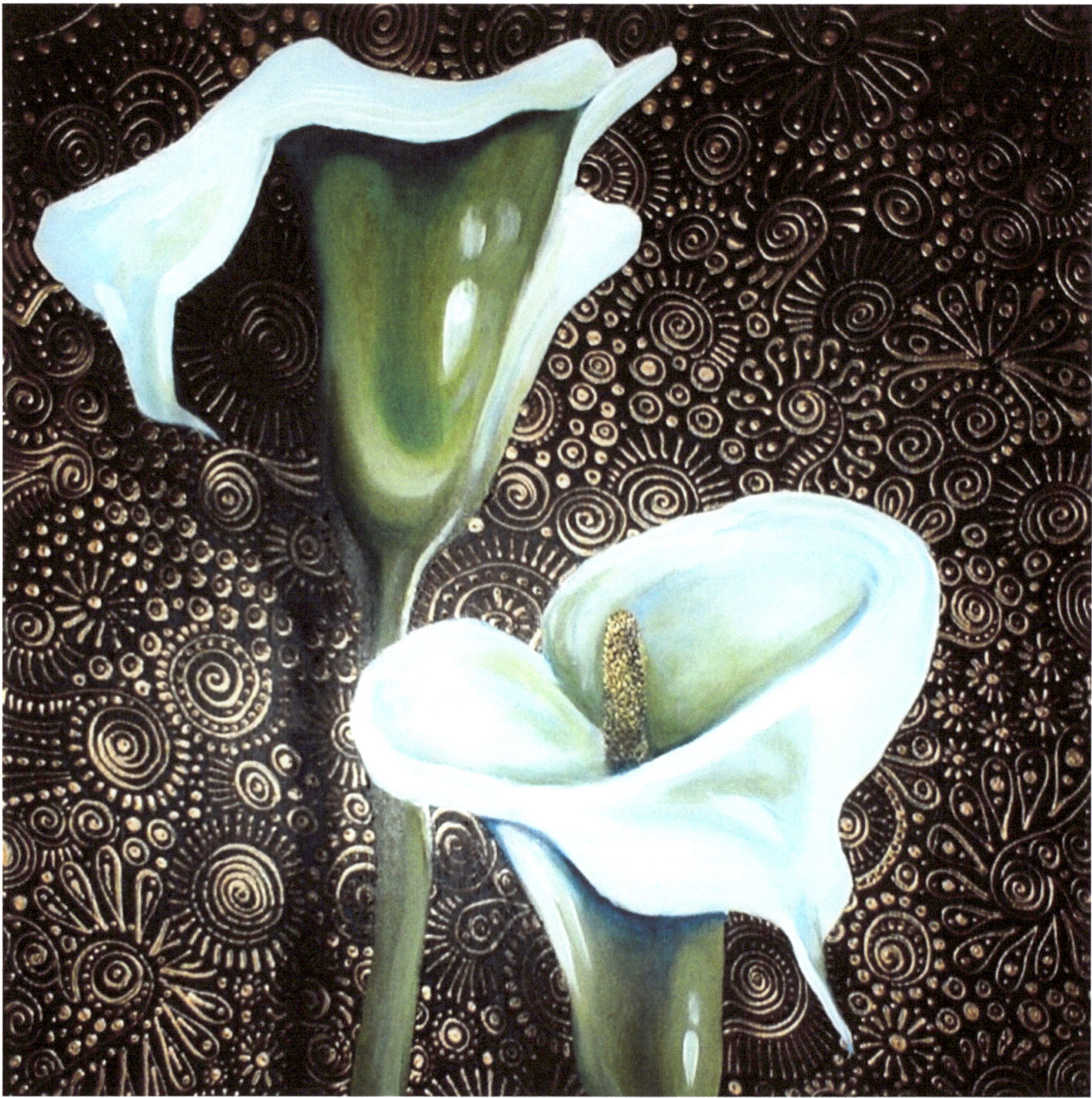

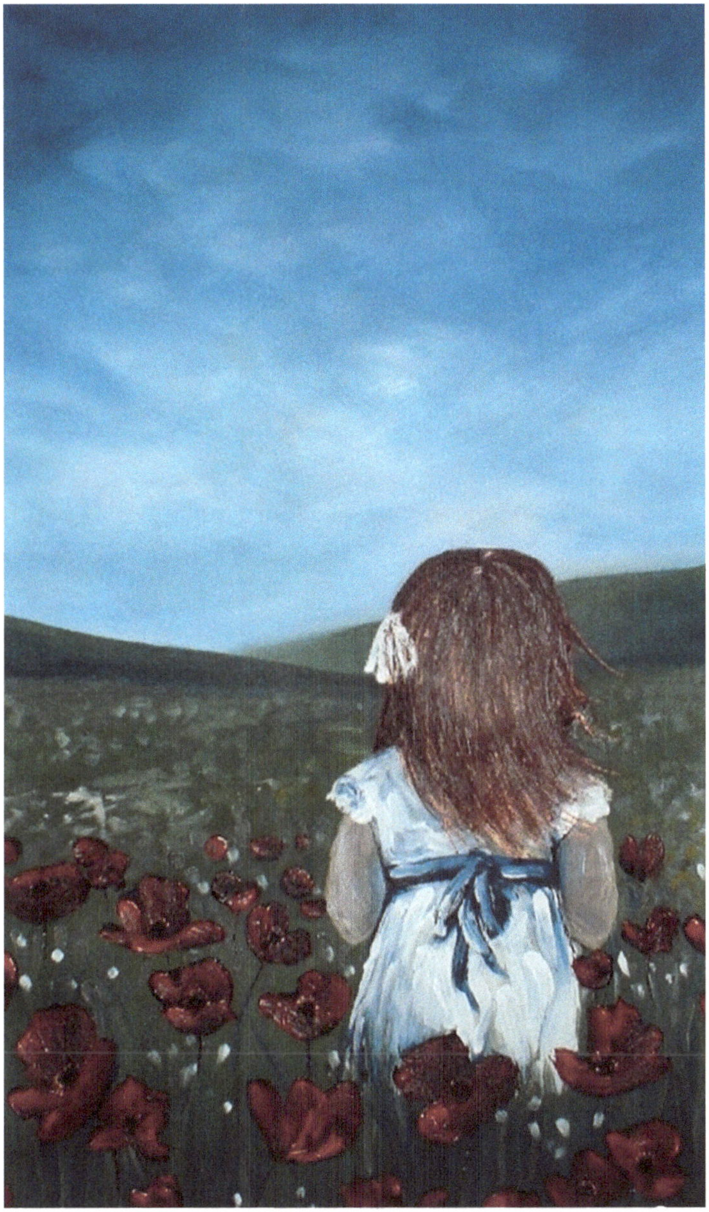

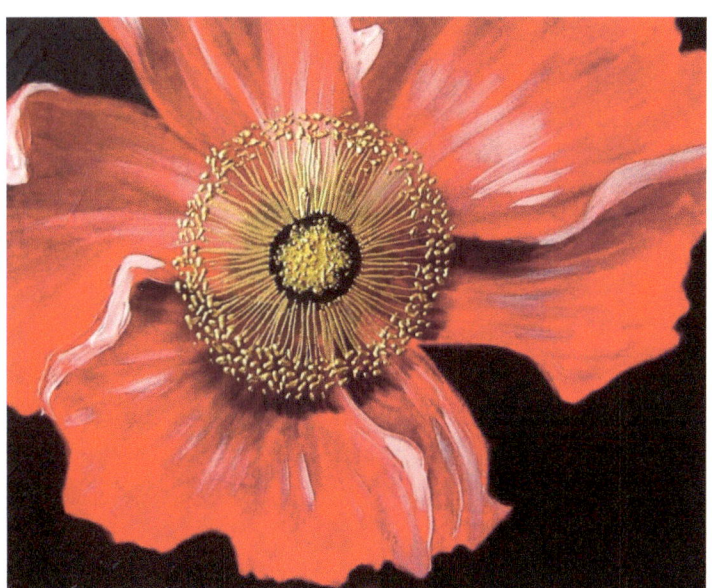
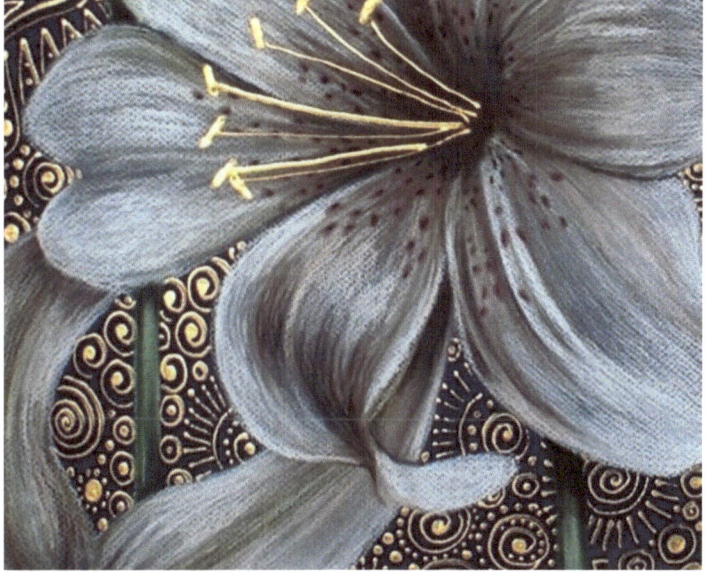

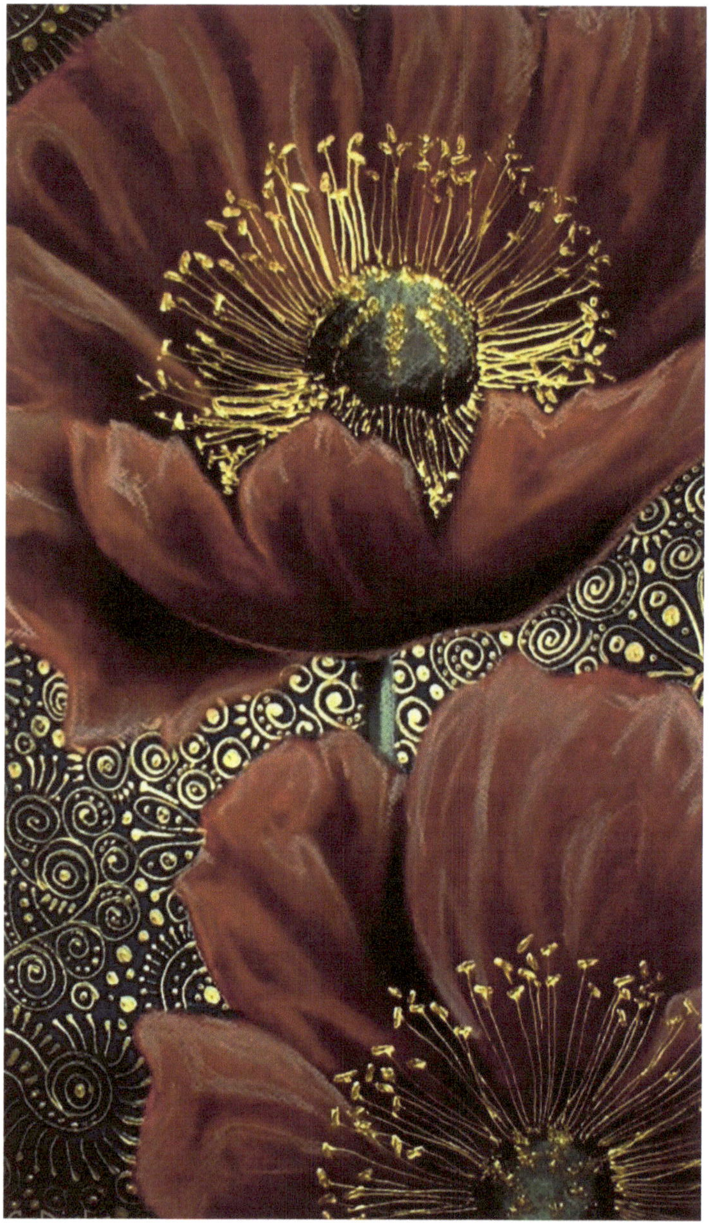

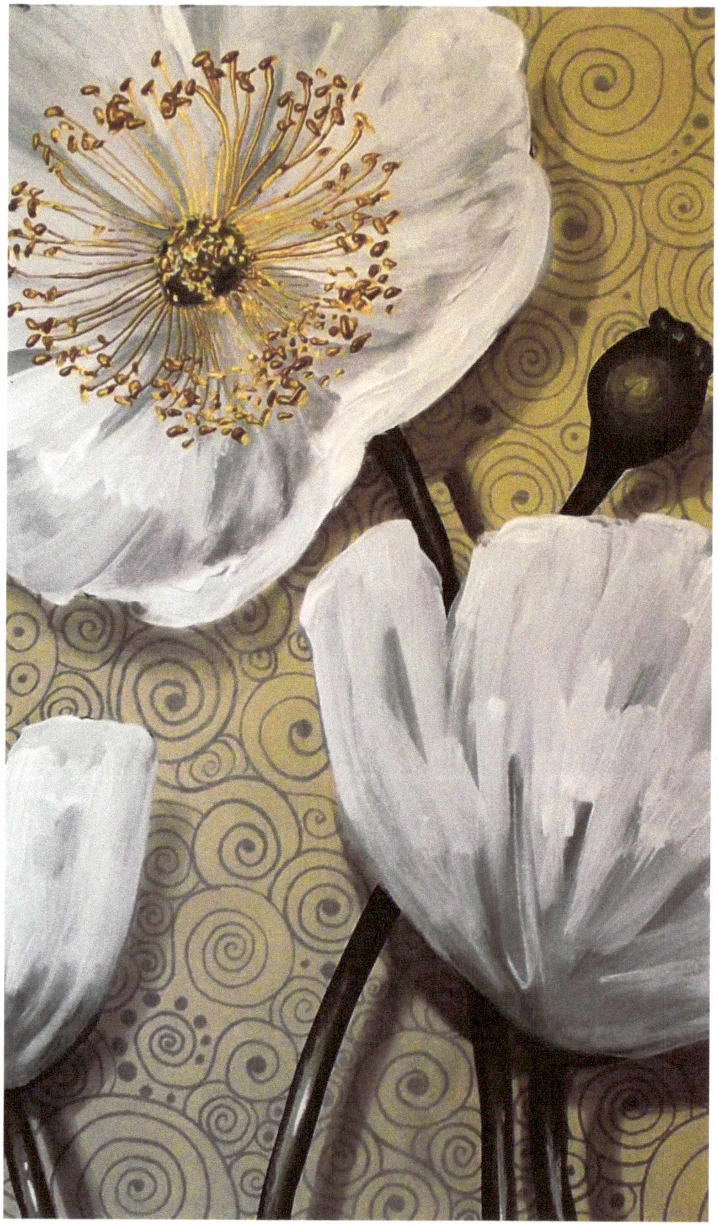

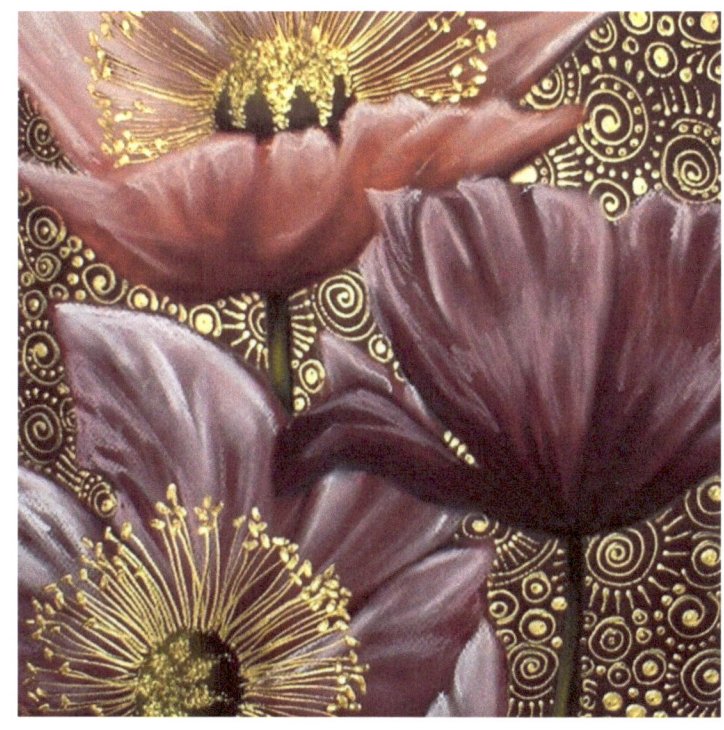

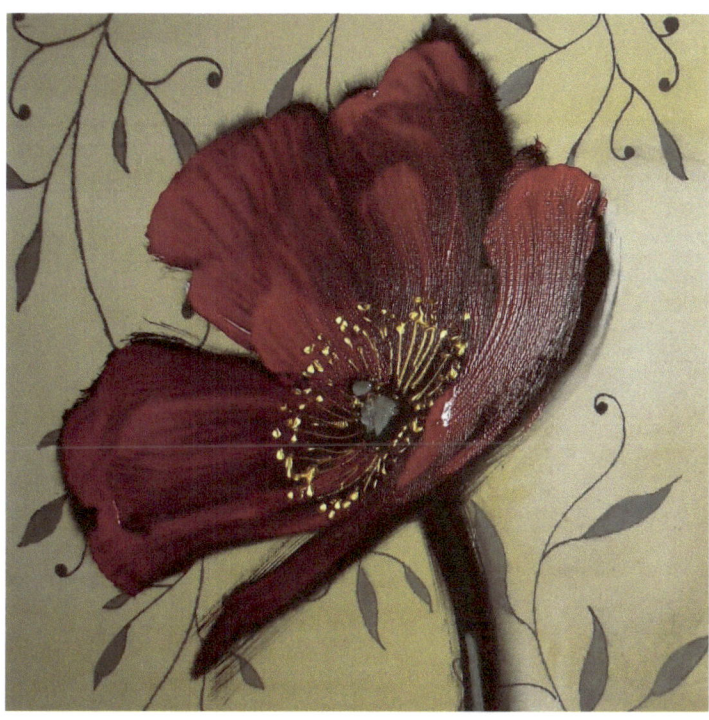

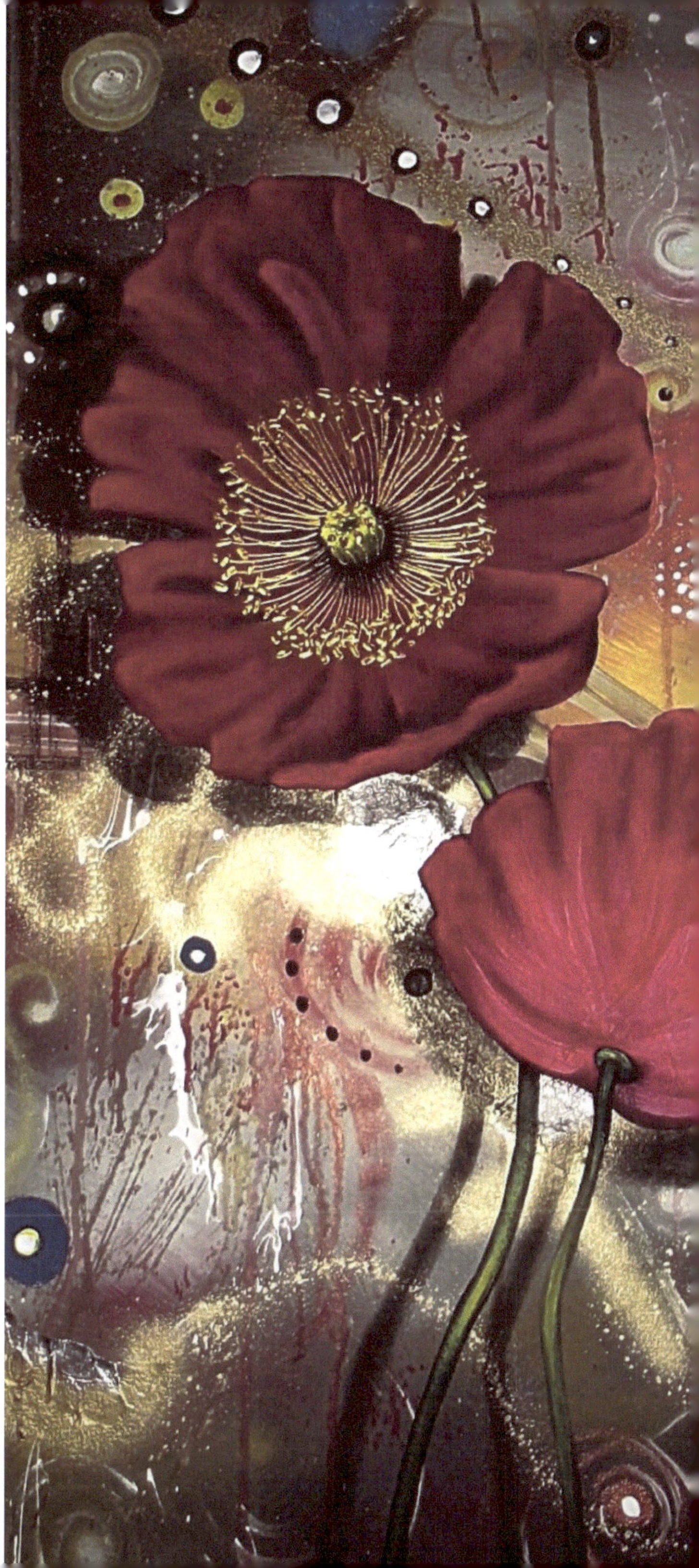

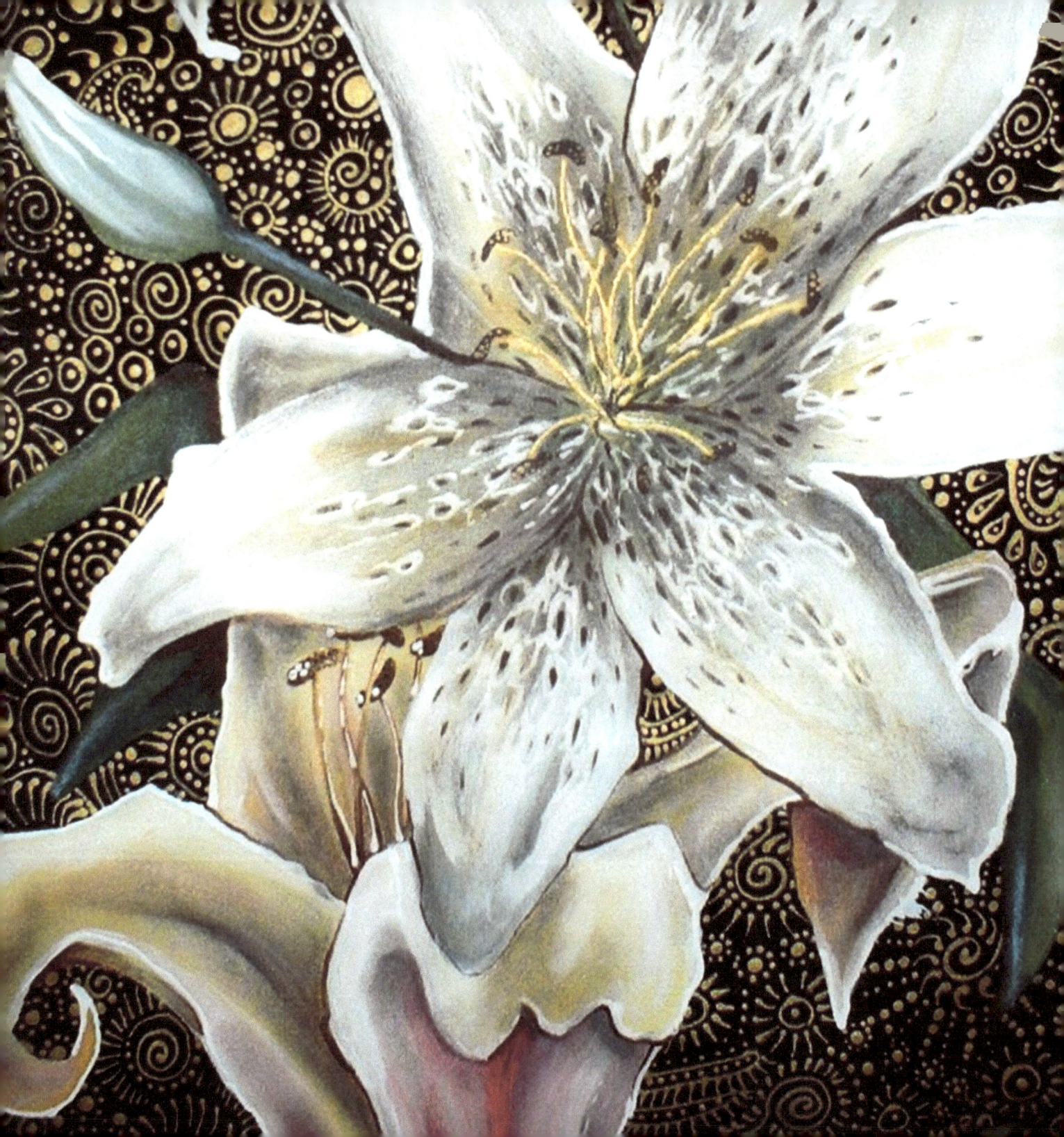

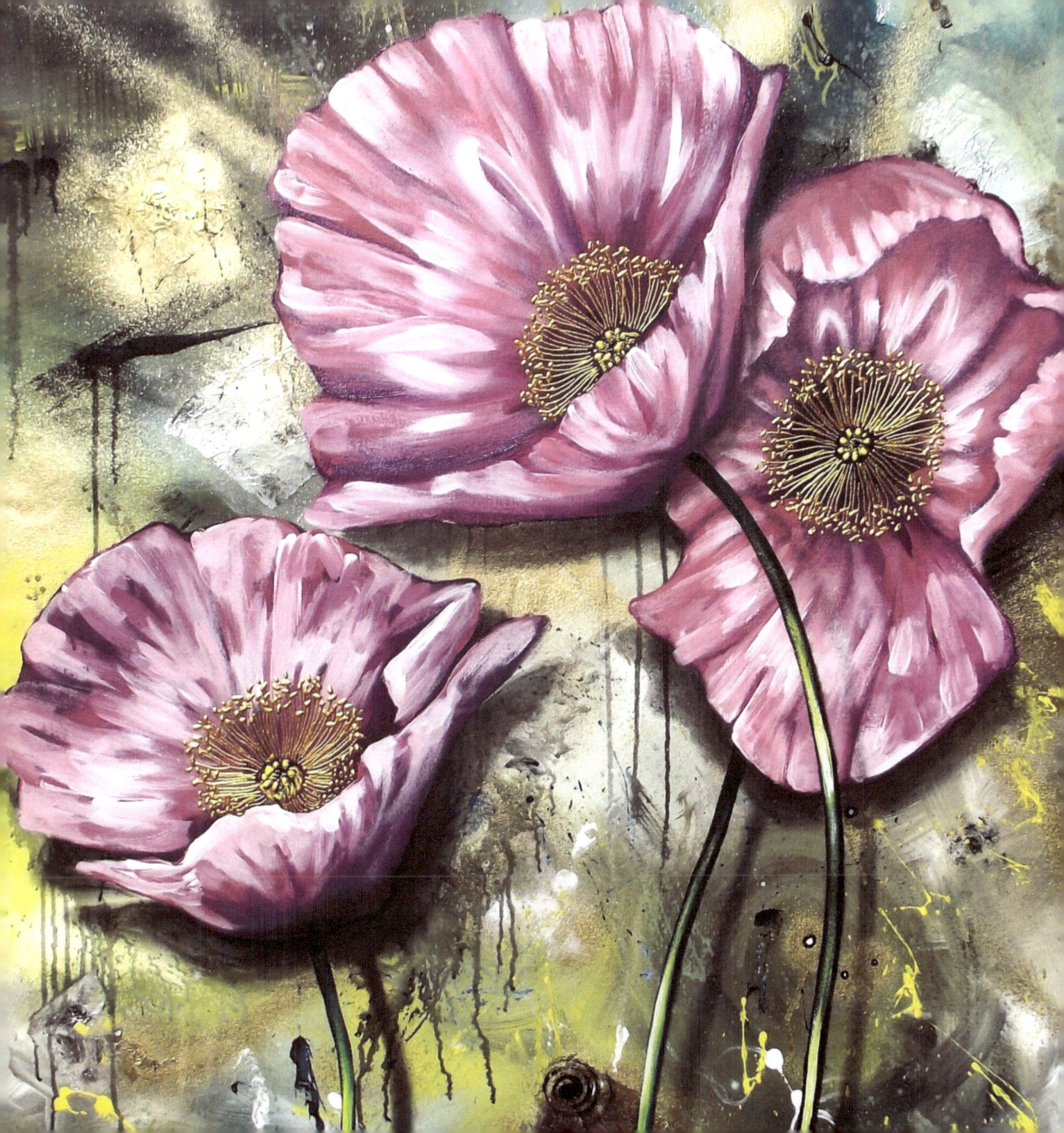

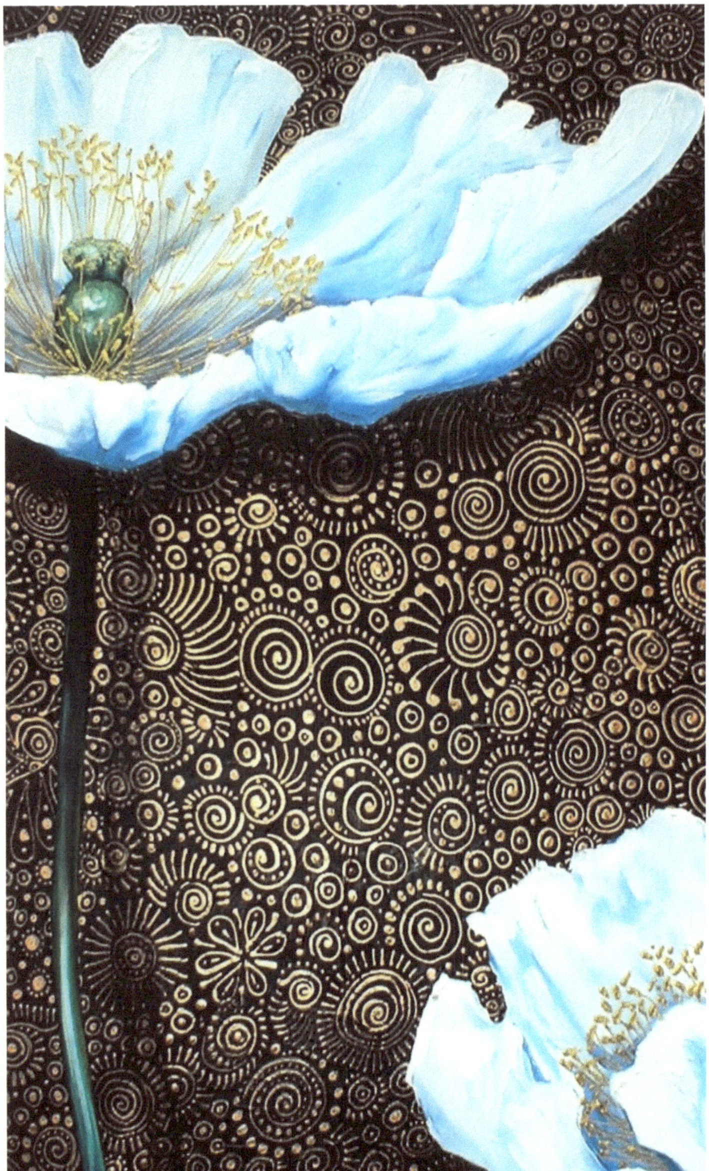

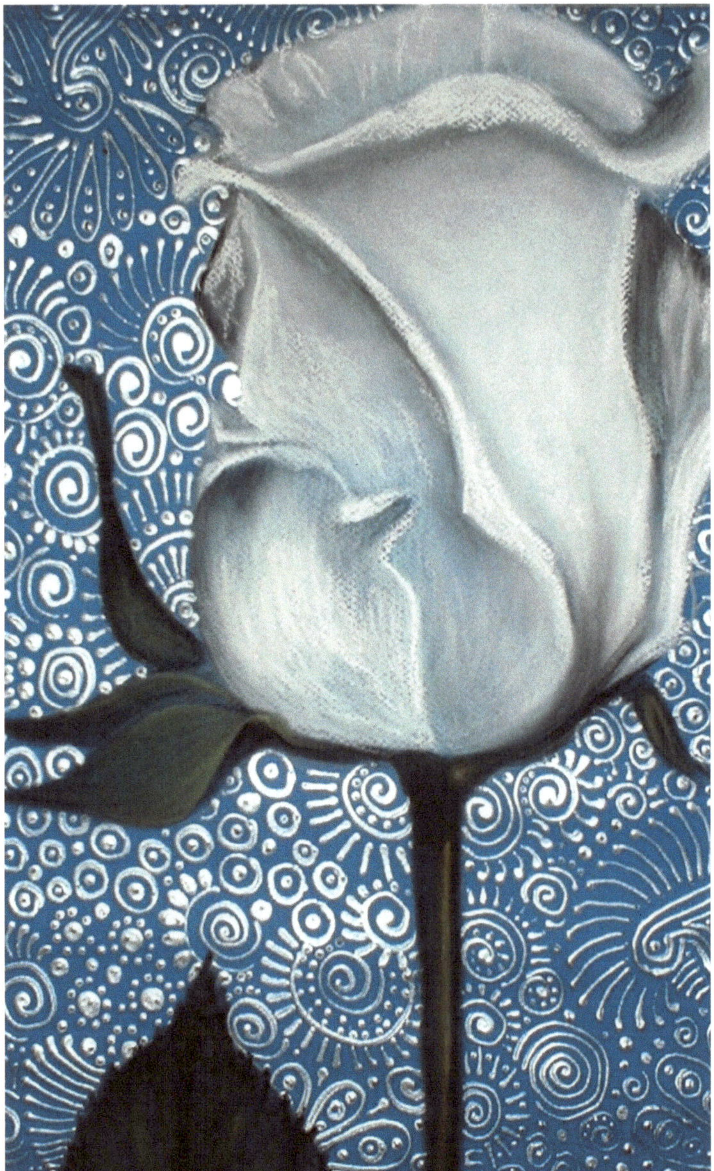

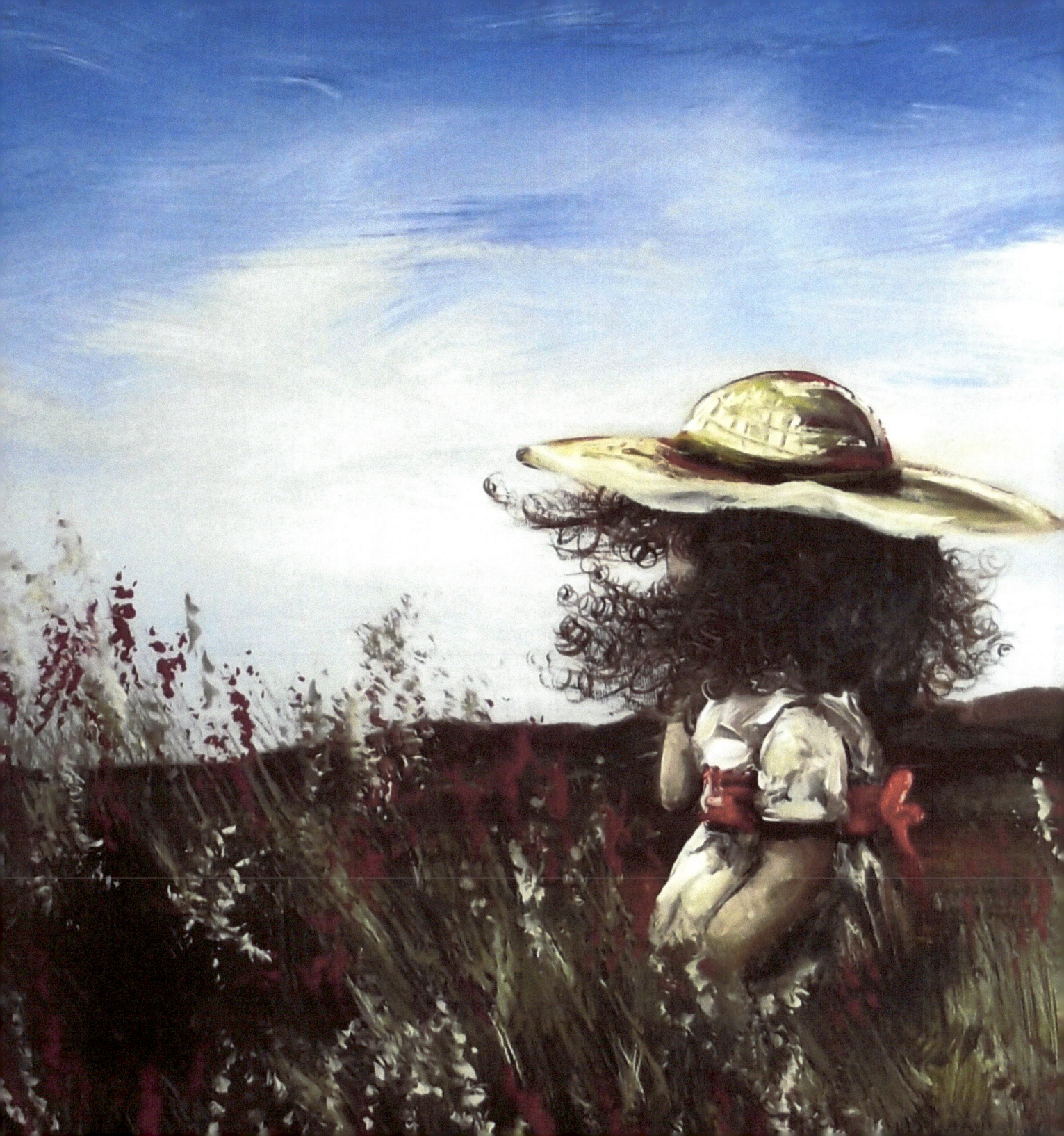

LANDSCAPES AND SEASCAPES

Who can't feast their eyes on a magnificent sunset or stand amidst a forest and not be in awe?

I believe that every manifestation on this planet - be it in the form of a rising sun, a spectacular cloud formation, the power and serenity of the ocean, or a majestic, aged tree - is a blessing and how we use this inspiration is our way of paying it forward.

I sometimes feel tears of bliss forming when I am captivated by a colour explosive sunset. We are all Gods playing in the illusory field of matter. I want to put on the best damn theatrical production I can! Make the sunsets and landscapes the best backdrops a playwright could ever dream of. I don't want to let a single sunset go unnoticed. Look out into this fantastic world and see the fields of colour and movement. Look up into the branches of a tree and feel the life that it possesses.

This is life on Earth and I love every second of it...

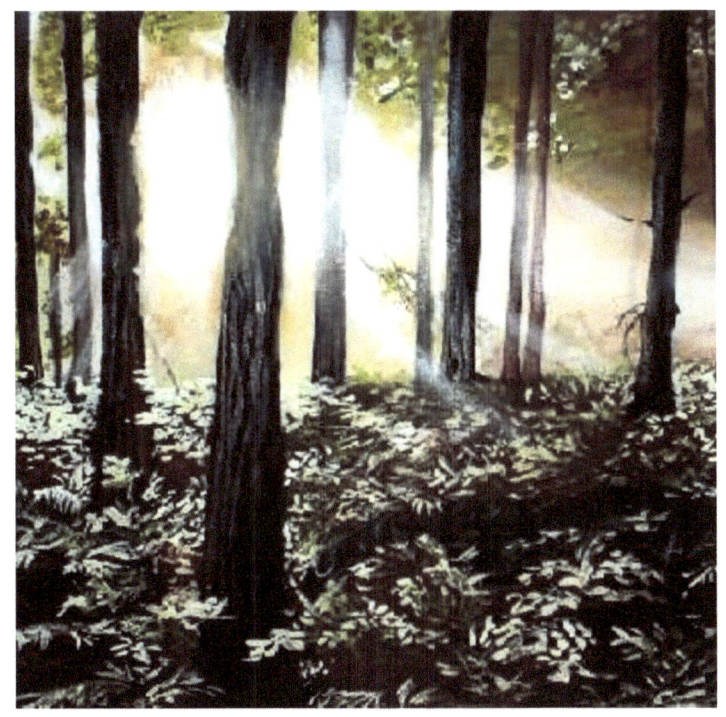

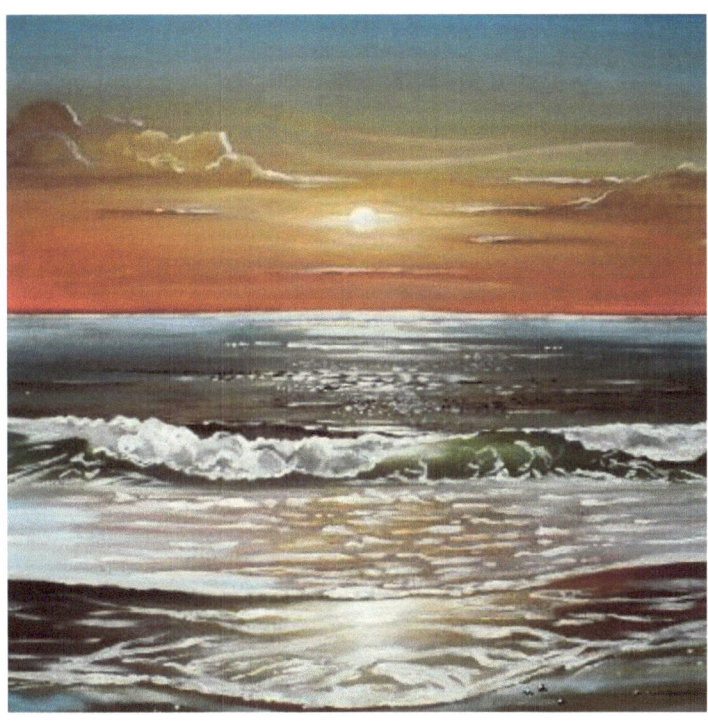

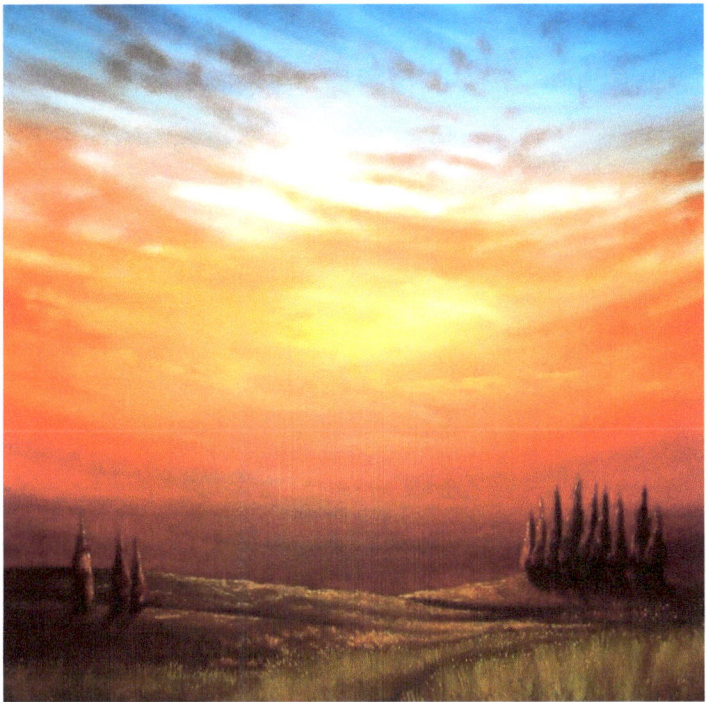

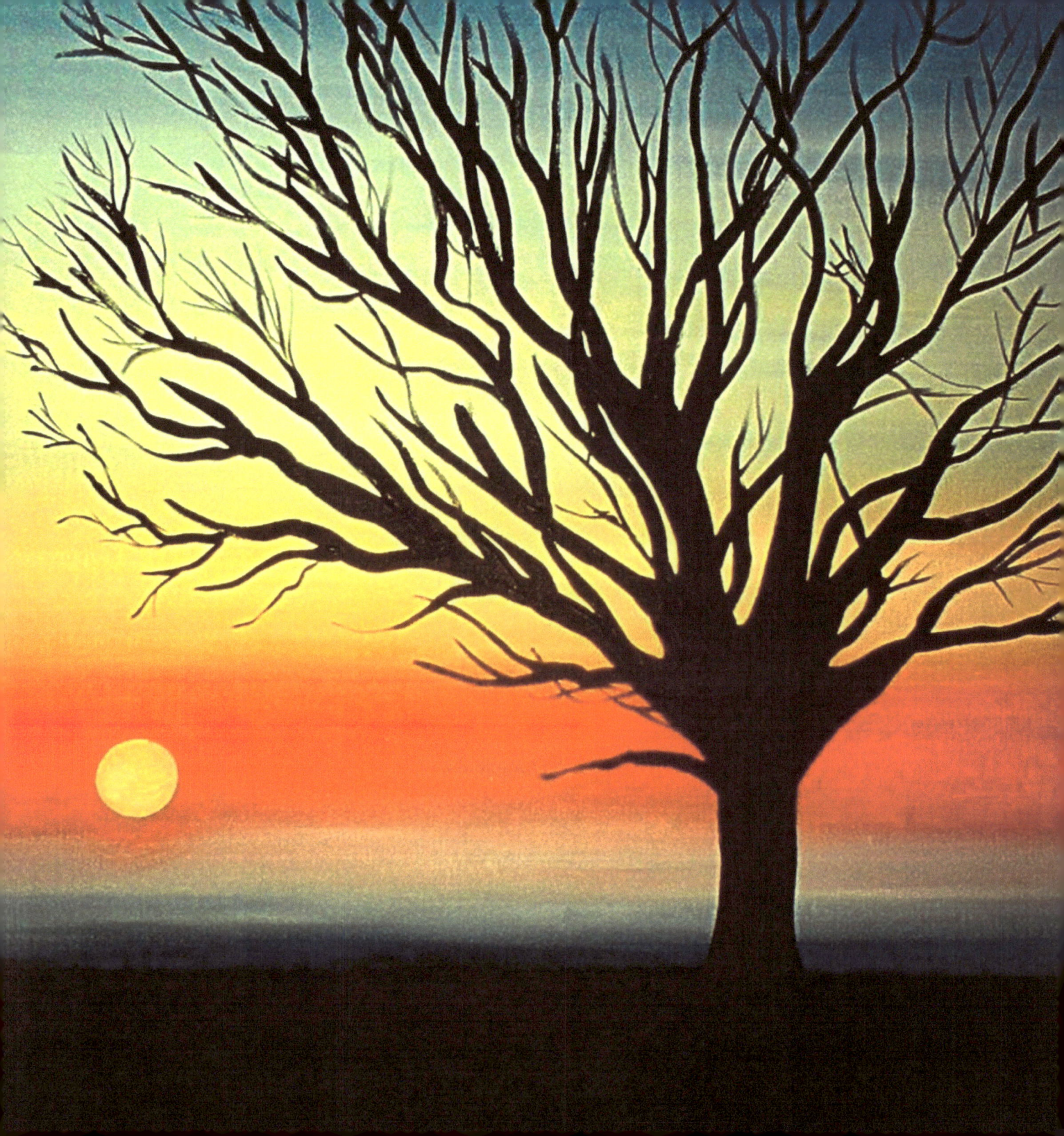

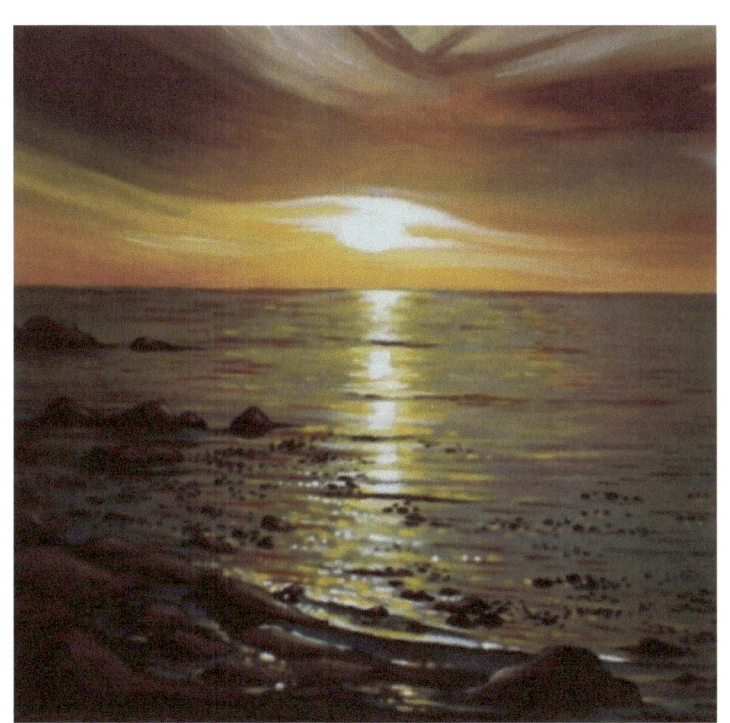

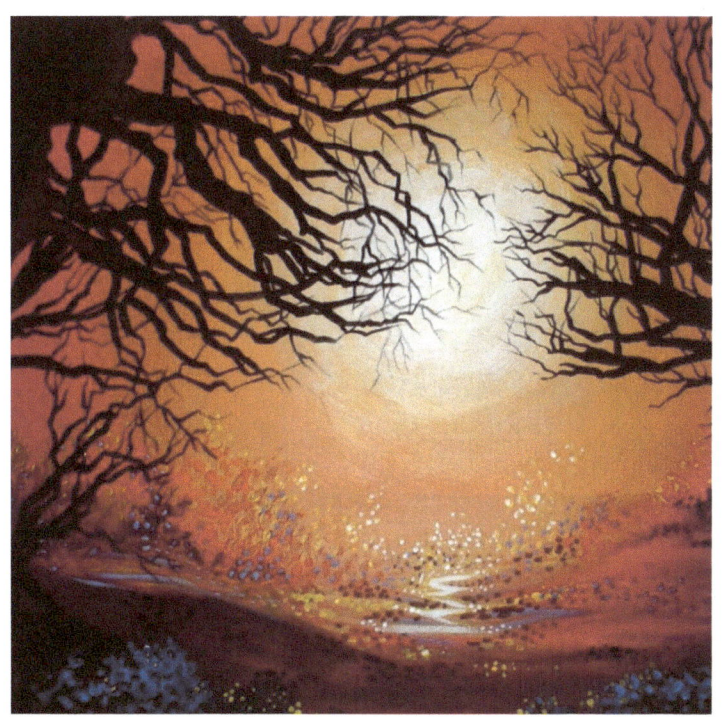

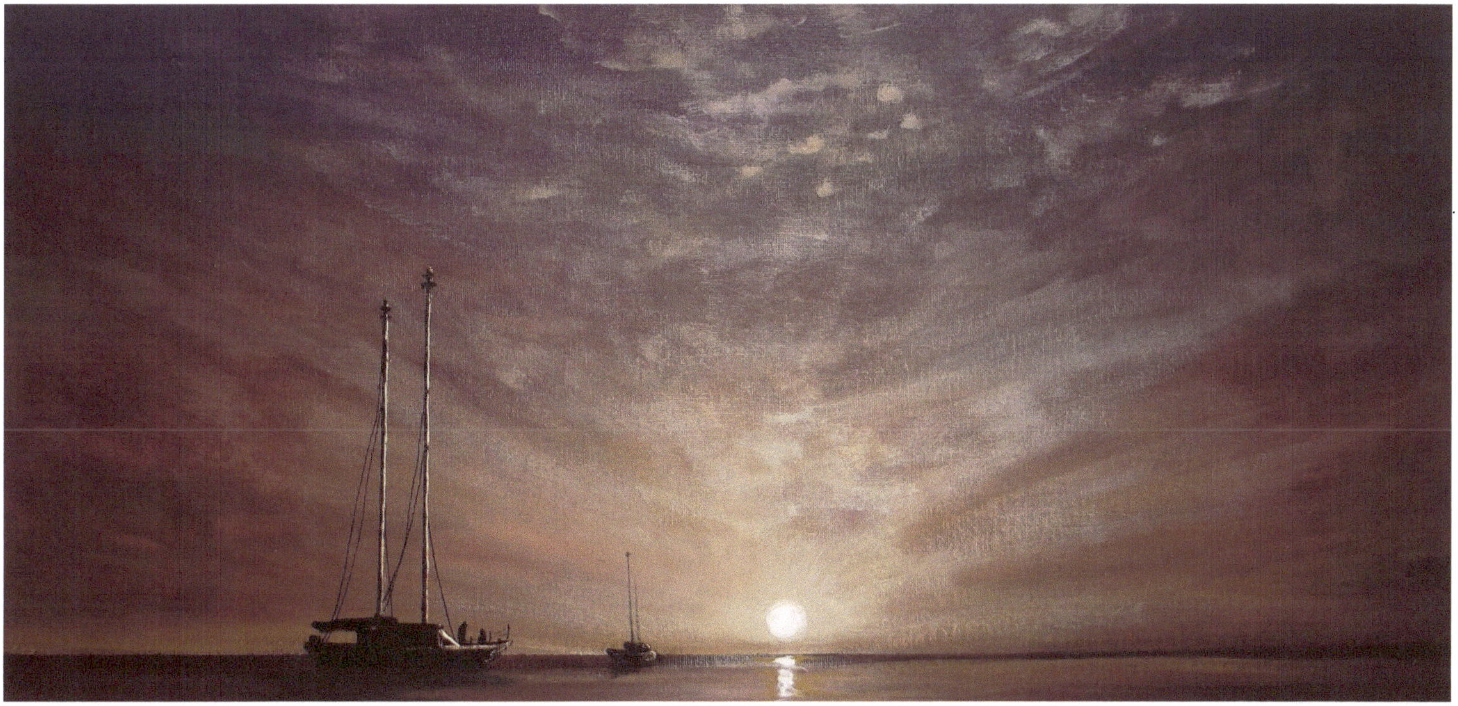

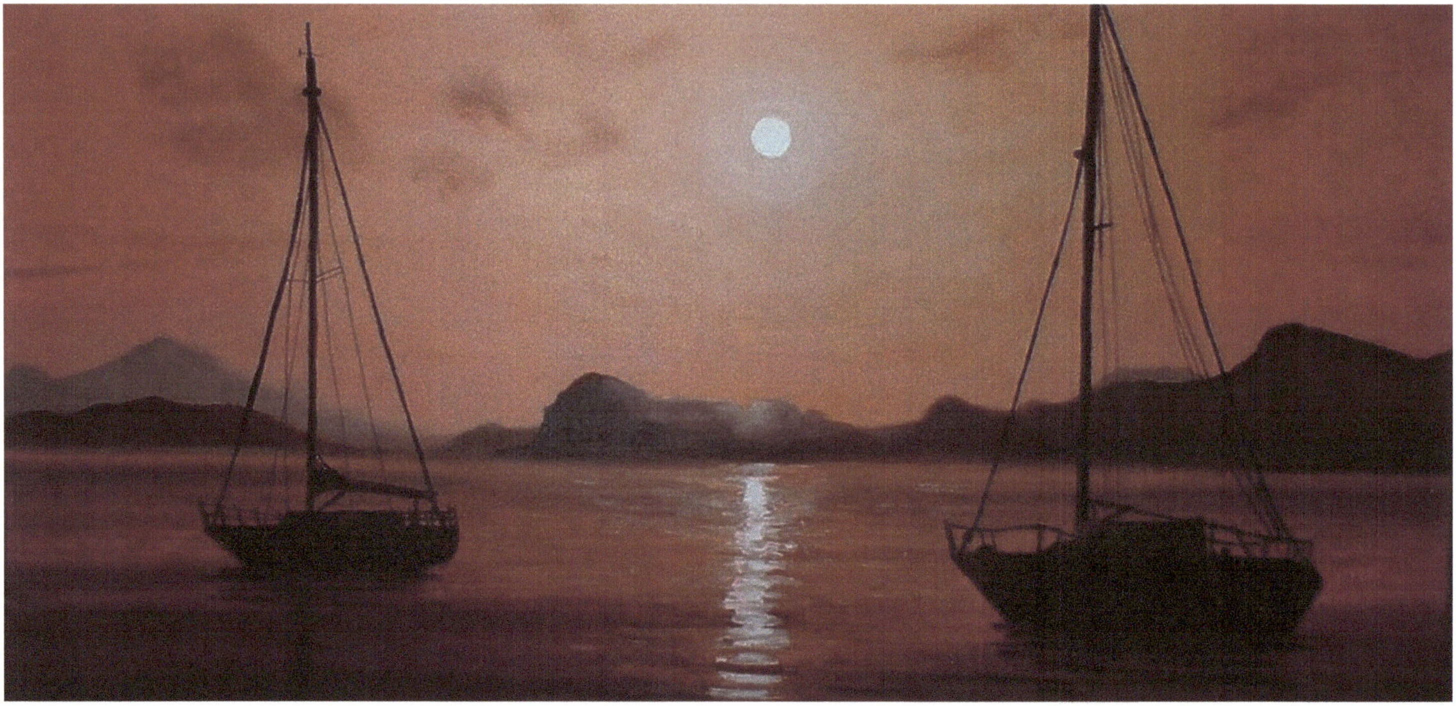

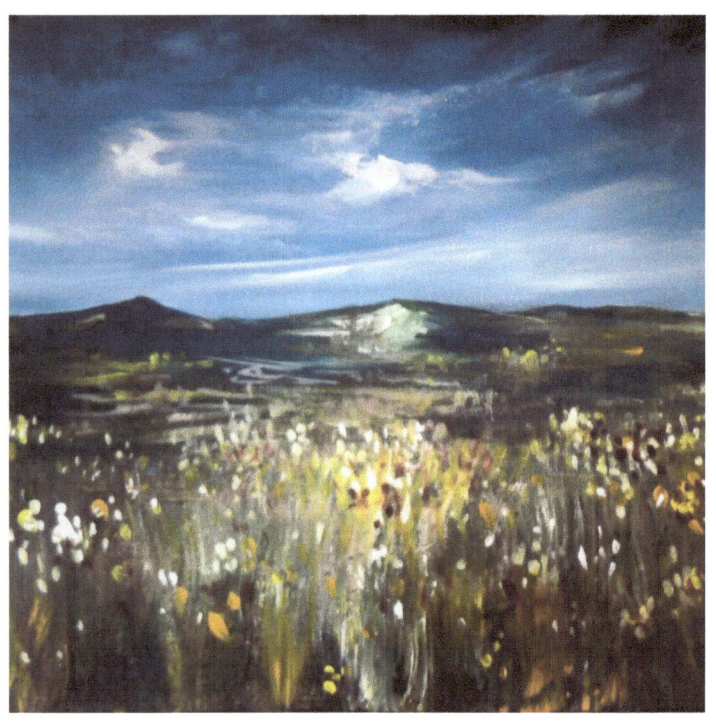
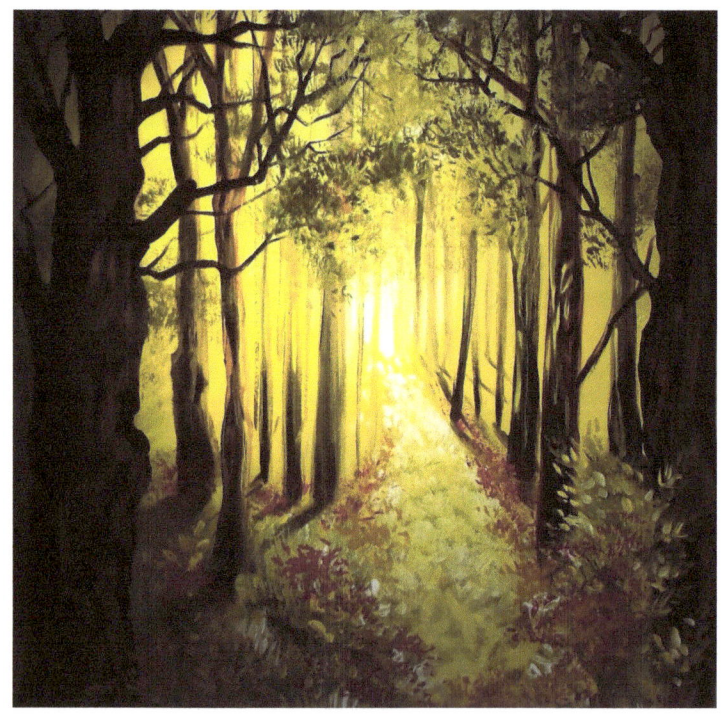

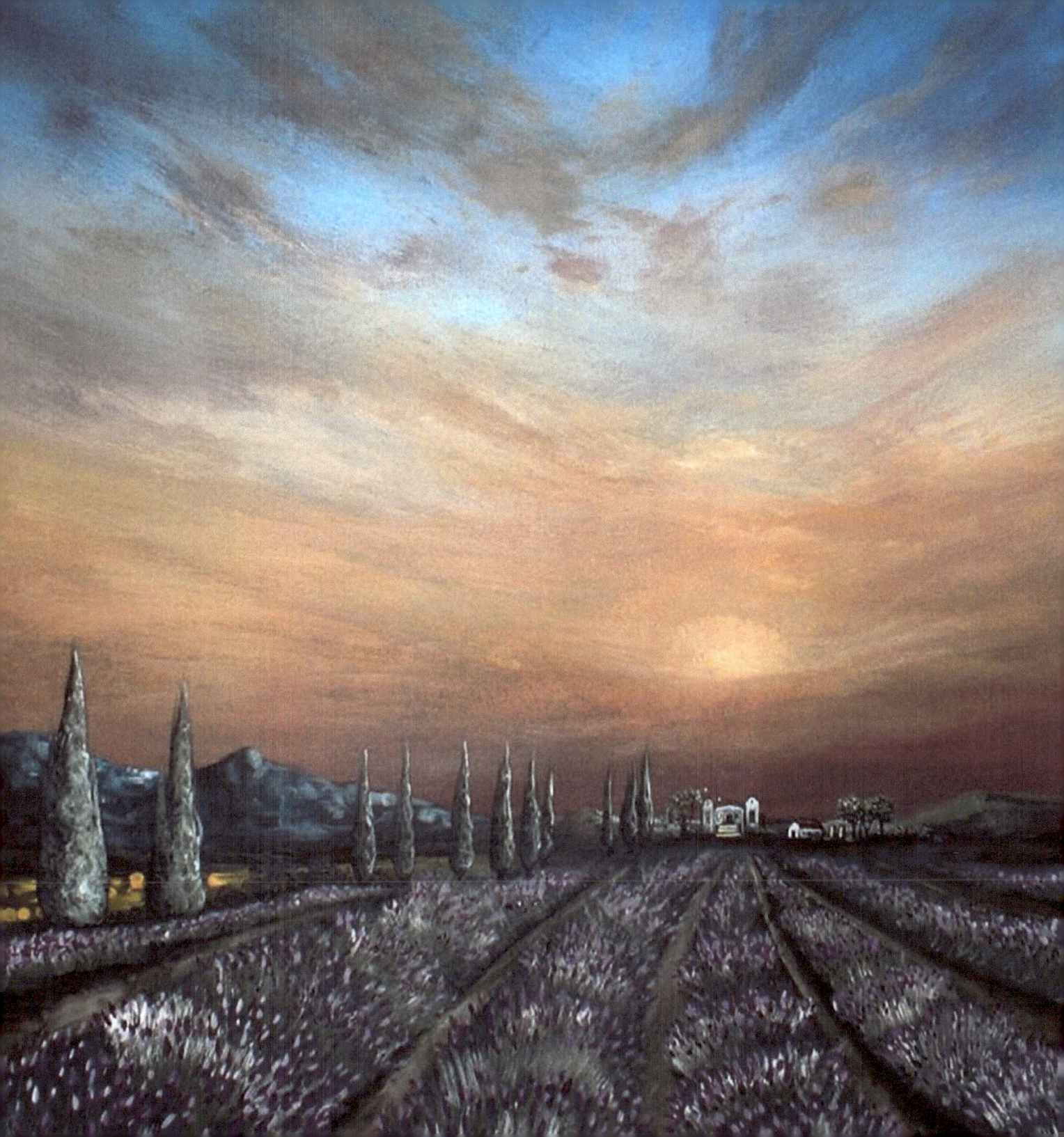

ANIMAL PLANET

I feel privileged and humble to share the planet with the incredible animal kingdom. Every single living entity has a character, uniqueness and beauty all of its own. No creature, big or small, is undeserving of appreciation. I strive to capture their essence of power, magnificence and grace in my work.

Having pets of my own, I am always moved by their unconditional love and ability to ground me in the present moment. Animals touch the heart and keep us on our toes at the same time!

They are here to help us in so many ways. Most of all, they are good at opening our heart chakra which shows us how to live from the heart centre as opposed to only operating with the mind.

Animals are such an enigma, some people wonder if they have a soul or not - for me there is no debate. Look into the eyes of an animal and you will find your answer. Like I said before, we share the planet with these wonderous beings and they deserve our respect, love and gratitude.

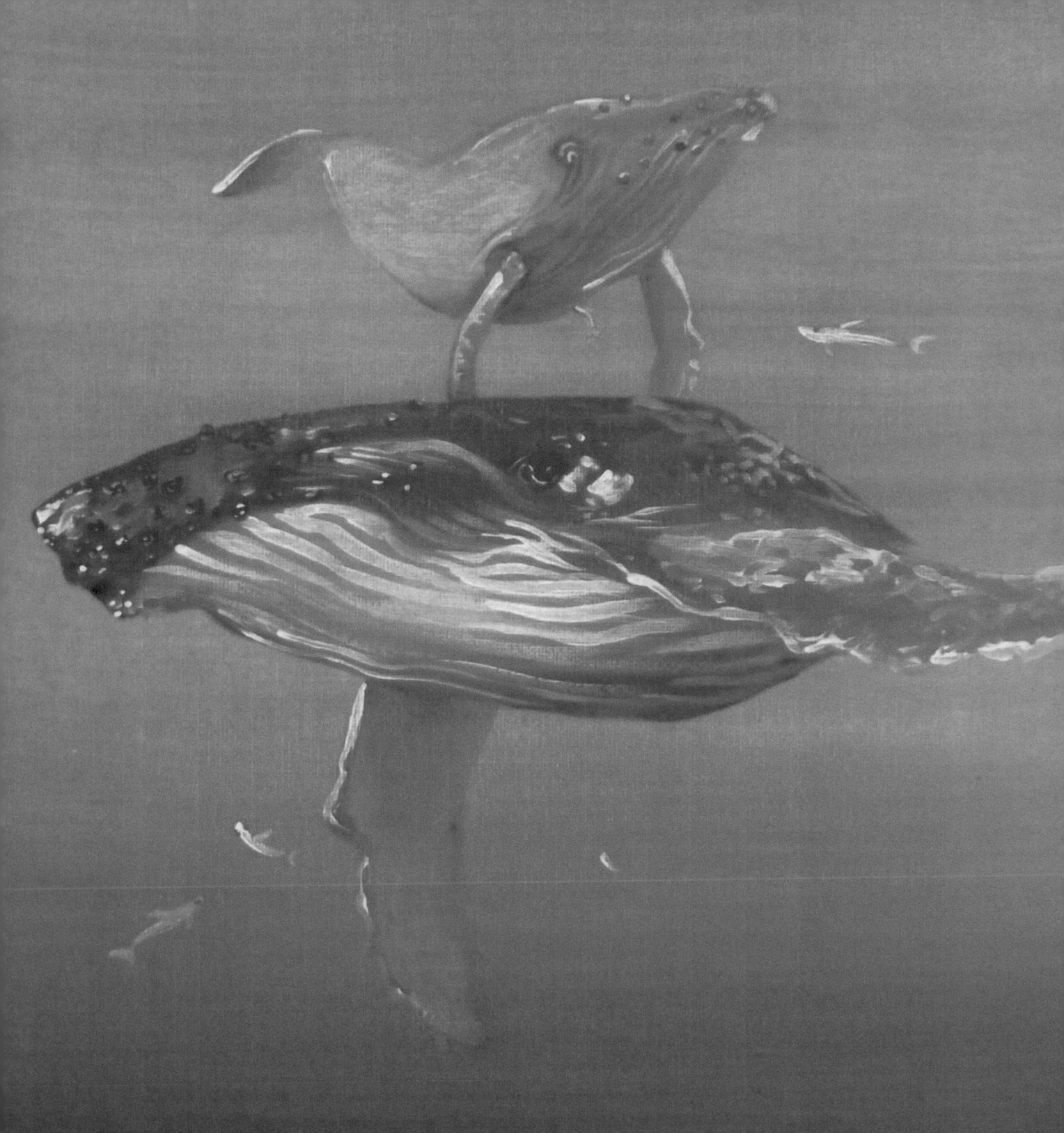

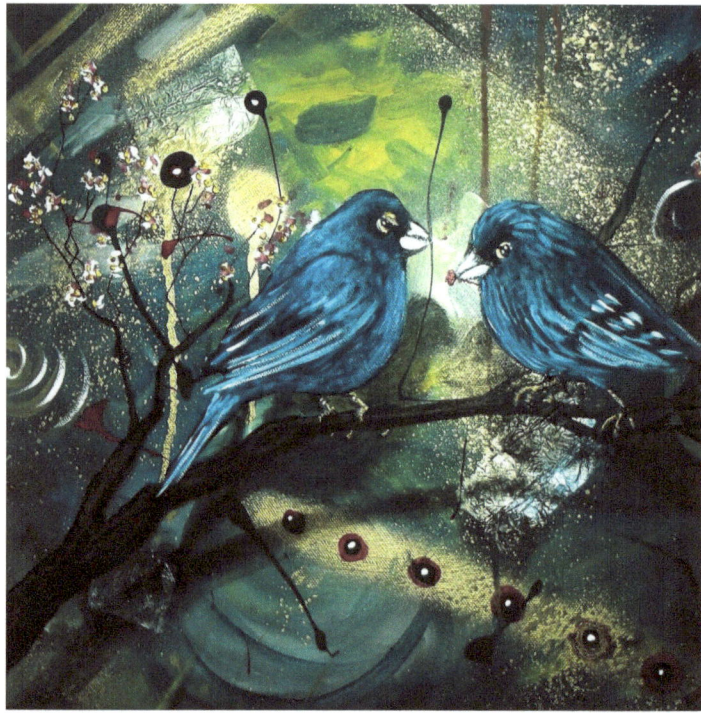

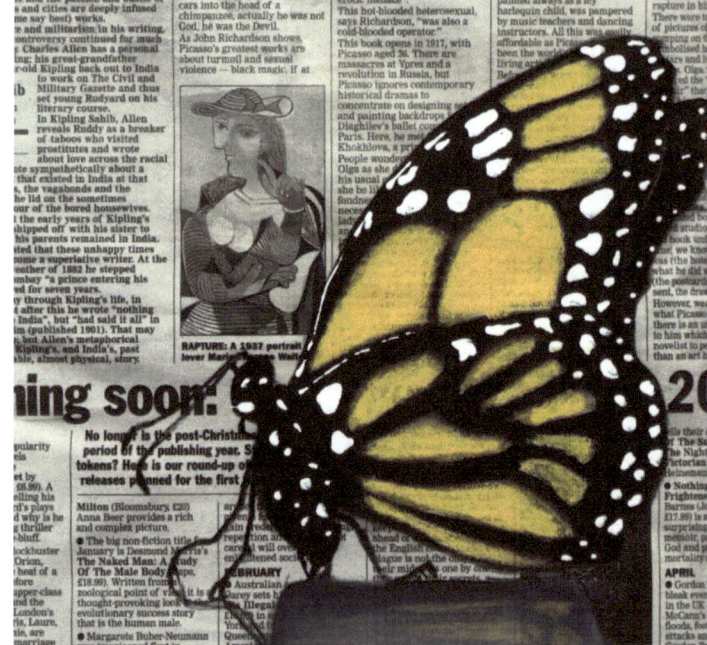

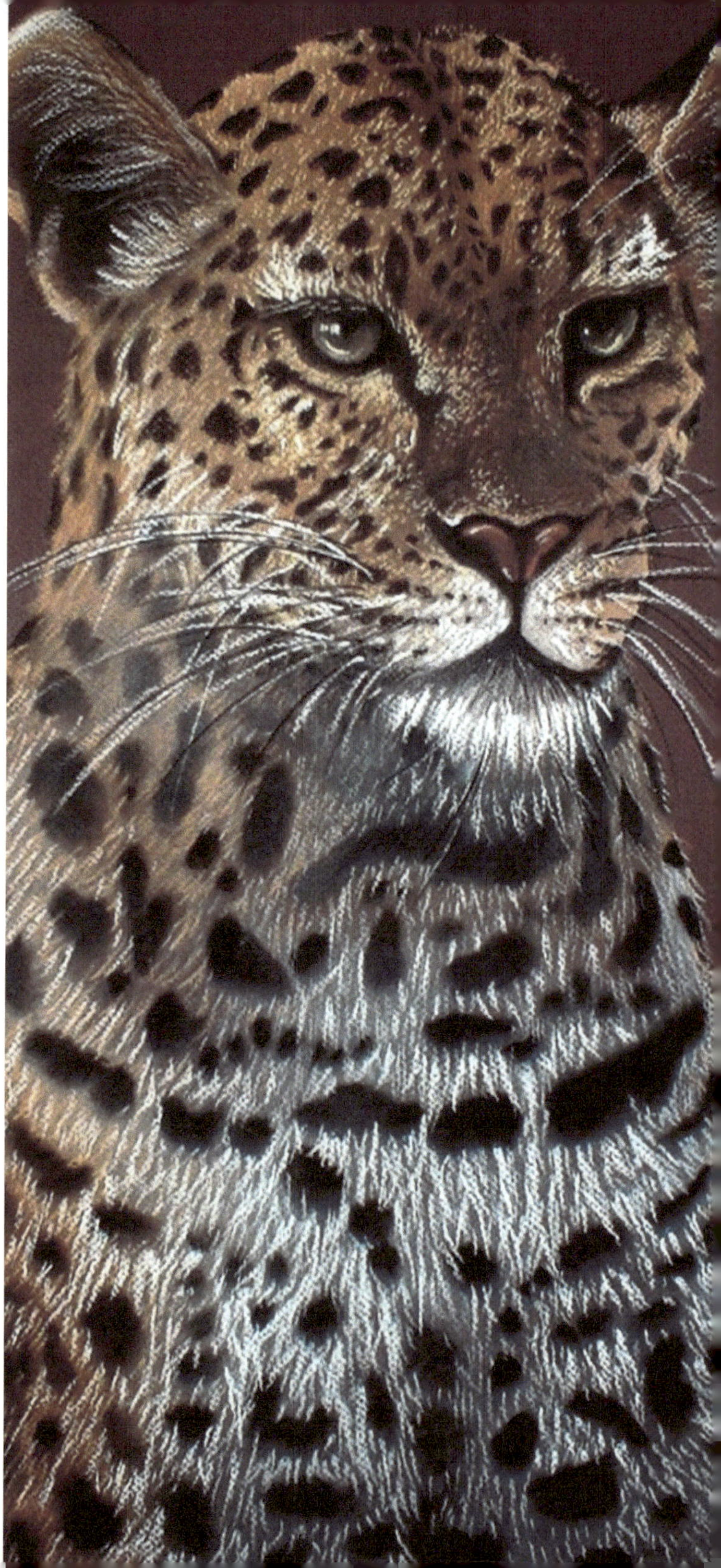

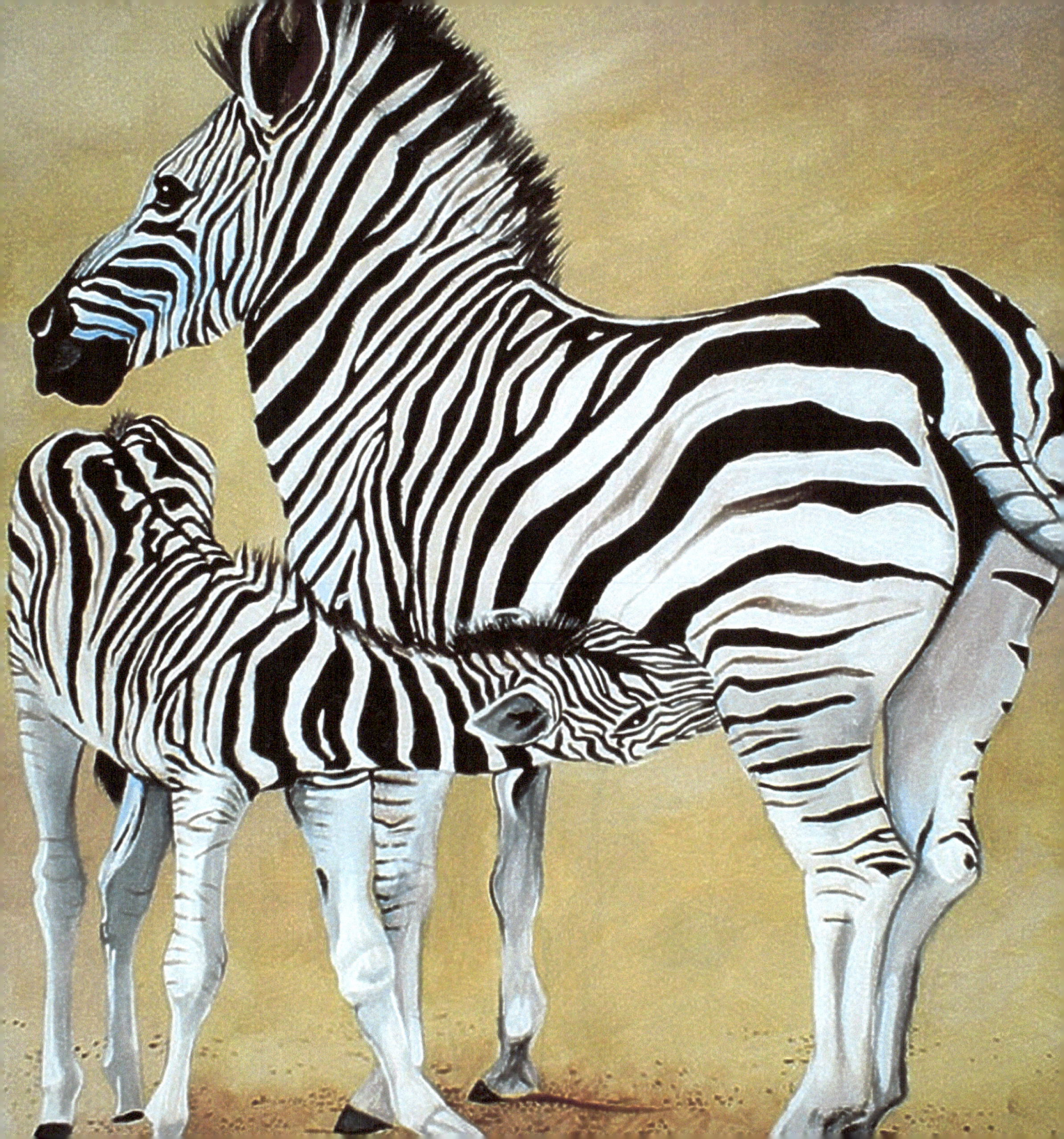

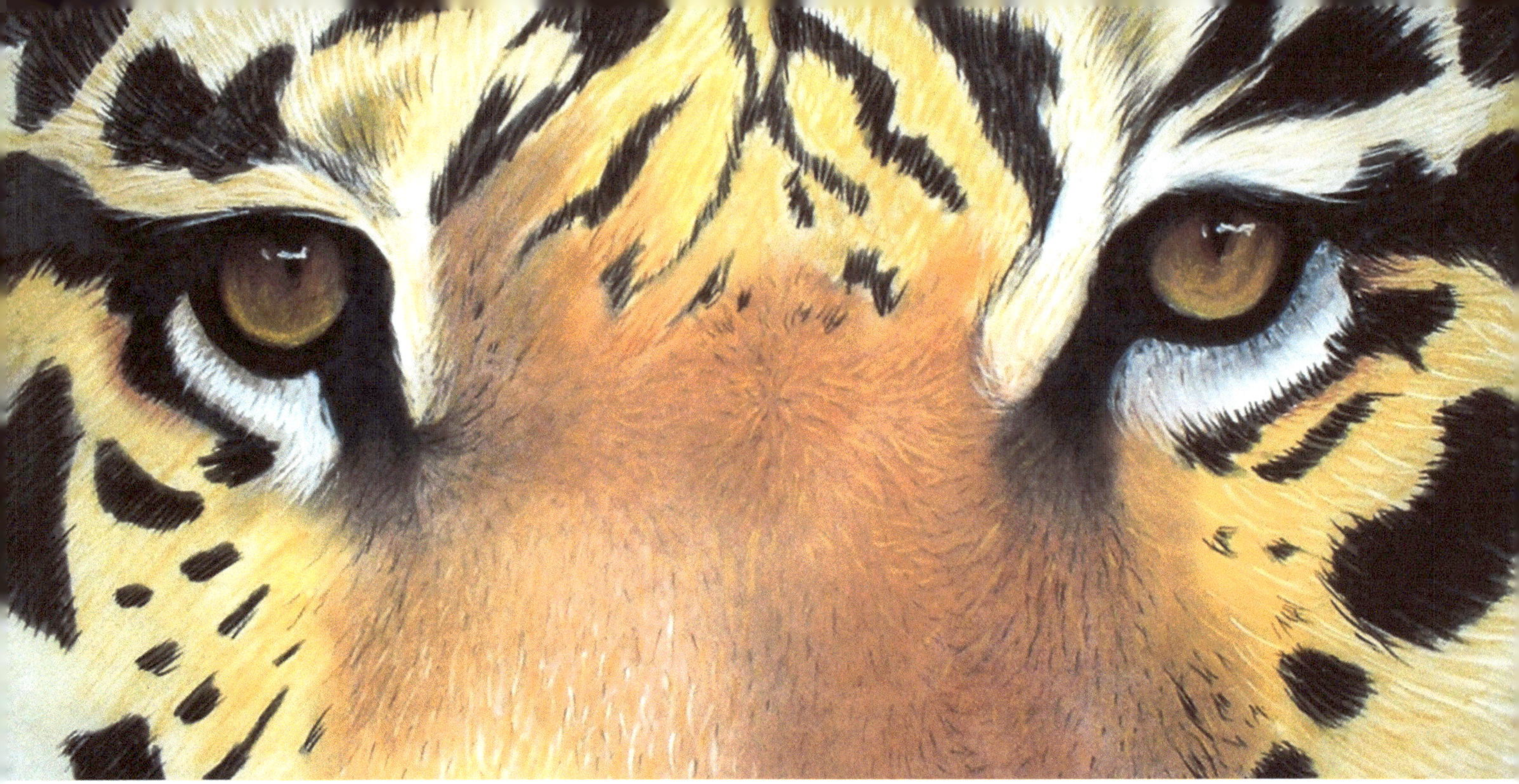

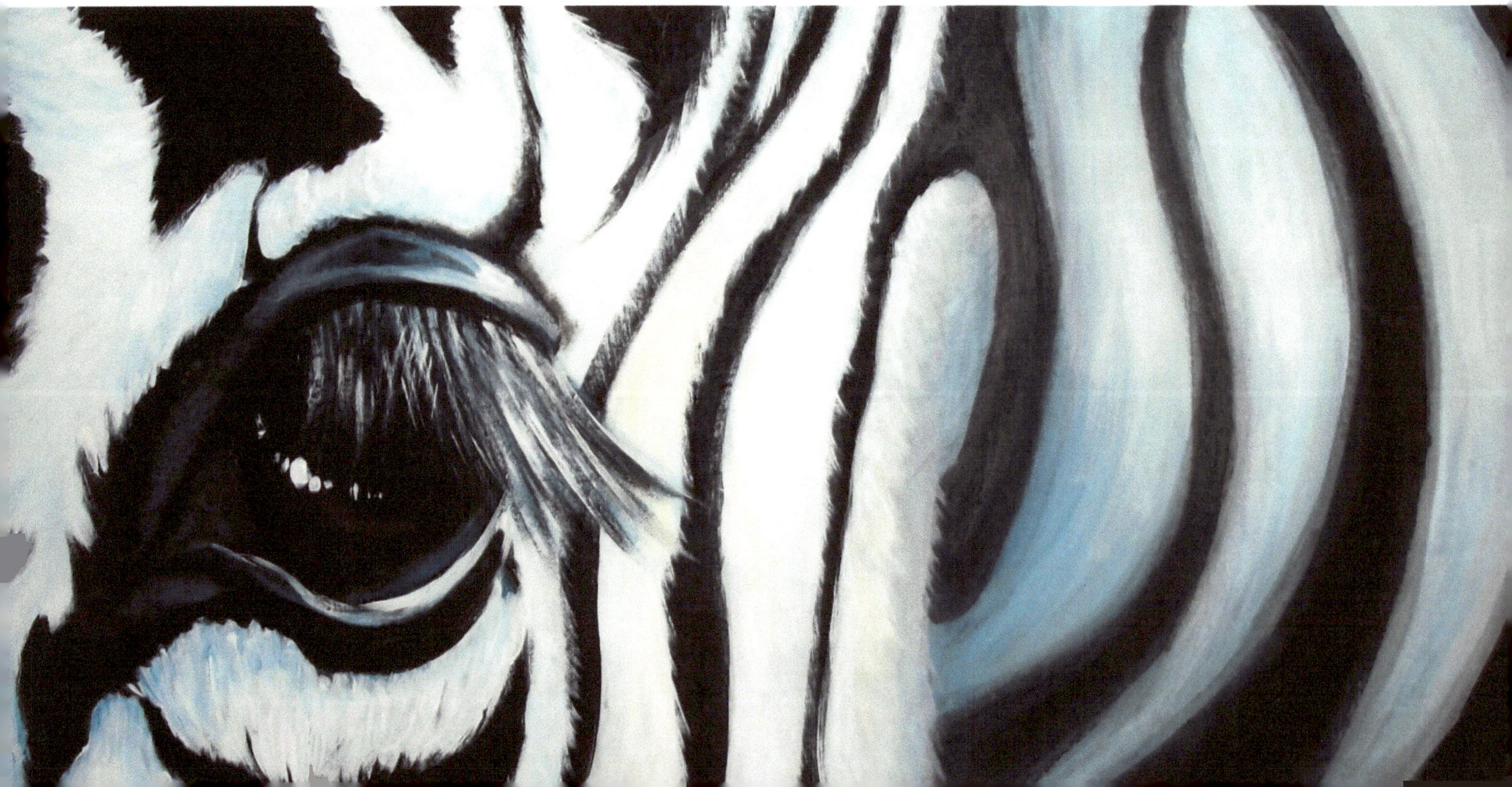

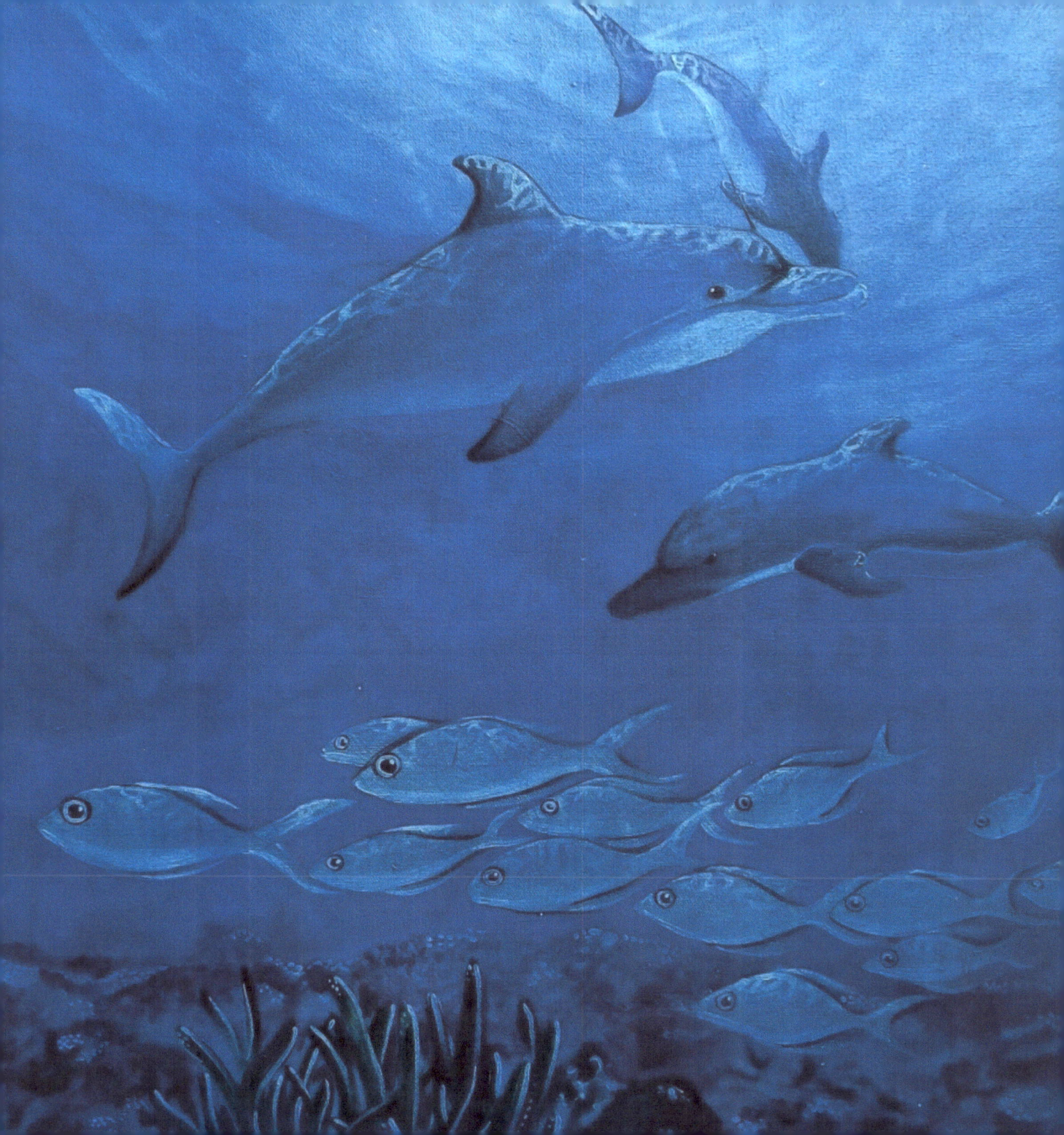

www.ingramcontent.com/pod-product-compliance
Lightning Source LLC
Chambersburg PA
CBHW050431180526
45159CB00005B/2500